THE LITTLE BOOK OF GREEN TIPS

WILLIAM FORTT

THE LITTLE BOOK OF GREEN TIPS

WILLIAM FORTT

Absolute Press

First published in Great Britain in 2007 by
Absolute Press
Scarborough House, 29 James Street West
Bath BA1 2BT, England
Phone 44 (0) 1225 316013 **Fax** 44 (0) 1225 445836
E-mail info@absolutepress.co.uk
Web www.absolutepress.co.uk

A catalogue record of this book is available from the British Library

ISBN 13: 9781904573630

Printed and bound in Italy by Legoprint

'This curious world which we
inhabit is more wonderful than it
is convenient, more beautiful
than it is useful.'

Henry David Thoreau

1

Act now. Take a thorough gimlet-eyed look at your lifestyle and see how you can make it more environmentally responsible. Turn that vague feeling of guilt into a positive and logical set of decisions which will help you to lead a greener existence.

2

Believe that you can make a difference.

Changing lightbulbs and recycling tin cans may seem like piffling gestures in the face of the world's gigantic environmental problems, but they do have an effect. More important still, they show that you care, and that you are involved.

3

Switch off as many lights as possible.

That includes outside lights, lights in rooms you're not using and unnecessary ceiling lights. Get into the habit of checking. This will not only cut your electricity bills, but also reduce light pollution in your neighbourhood.

4

If you can't drive less, at least **drive more slowly.** On open unrestricted roads, the optimum speed for economic fuel consumption is around 55 mph. Once you get up to 70 mph, you are using roughly 30% more fuel. Statistics show that slower driving is also safer.

5

Take your own bags to the shops. Buy a couple of good cloth bags, or a backpack, and use them to carry your shopping home. Shun the menace of the plastic bag which is usually made from petrochemical derivatives, and will end up in a landfill, hanging from a tree, or choking some poor sea creature.

6

Change to a 'green fund' electricity supplier. These companies still supply electricity from the National Grid. However, they plough the money from your bills into new, generally small-scale, renewable energy schemes, such as watermills and wind farms.

7

Check where your food has come from.

Look especially at the sources of fruit and vegetables to find their country of origin, and buy those which have come the shortest distance. The further a truck or cargo ship has to travel, the more pollution it causes and the more energy it uses.

8

Aim for an empty dustbin

– it is just about possible. The less you throw away, the less land gets used for burying rubbish. Leave unnecessary packaging at the store, recycle anything recyclable, rot down anything rottable (see #15) and reuse plastic bags and bottles.

9

Banish junk mail. Vast amounts of wood and water are wasted to produce unwanted advertising material which is never opened, let alone recycled. Sign up for the Mailing Preference Service, which will delete your address from national mailing lists.

10

Turn off electrical appliances when you're not using them. This applies especially to any with standby lights (on washing machines, cookers, DVD players, computers and a hundred other things). Even the tiniest light uses up electricity and is almost certainly unnecessary.

11

Buy a bicycle and use it.

Bike travel is brilliant exercise, and almost entirely non-polluting (bar the manufacturing process). 'Hybrid' bikes, a sort of halfway house between racers and mountain bikes, are ideal for most local journeys, being both comfortable and rugged.

12

Check your house insulation. Lost heat means needless waste and bigger heating bills. Has the loft been lined and insulated properly (with at least two layers)? Has the wall cavity been filled? Are there gaps in windows and doors?

13

Everyone knows that you can

recycle glass bottles, newspapers and tin cans. But what about more complicated bits of **hardware?**

Mobile phones, computer components and batteries all contain valuable ingredients which can be reused. Contact your local environment agency for specific advice.

14

Undecided about a screen saver on
your computer? Try a blank screen.

Simply **turn off the monitor when you're not using it.** Better still – programme your computer to shut down the monitor automatically during idle periods.

15

Build yourself a compost heap.

Big or small – they're all useful. Anything plant-based can go on it, including newspapers, vegetable waste, perennial weeds from the garden, wilted flowers, cardboard cartons and dead leaves. Chop everything up small with a sharp spade and turn the heap once or twice to mix the contents.

16

Put a brick in your lavatory cistern.

It will **save** you a brick's worth of **water every time you flush**

– which is a lot over a year. If you haven't a brick handy, then fill a plastic bottle with water, put on the cap and put that in the cistern. Make sure it doesn't get in the way of the ball valve mechanism.

17

Desperate to wash your car?

Make use of Mother Nature and

wait until it rains. Use the rainwater to remove the excess muck, and then to rinse off the waxing solution. You'll need some waterproofs yourself, though.

18

Get to know your local cycle paths, and buy cycle maps which show you the safest roads to ride on. The security of dedicated paths and tracks make them attractive for bicycling families, and give new riders a lot of confidence.

19

Put your baby in washable nappies. Millions of disposable nappies clog the sewers and take up a lot of landfill space. What's more, their manufacture causes pollution and uses valuable resources. And one baby will get through a tonne of them. Washable nappies are much cheaper and not that much extra work.

20

Switch off your car engine whenever possible. Idling in traffic jams or car parks uses up fuel, cokes up your engine and pumps out needless pollution. It sounds obvious – but a surprising number of people leave their engines running pointlessly. If it's cold, wear another coat.

21

Change your light bulbs for types which use less energy.

Look for Compact Fluorescent Lamps (CFLs) or Light-Emitting Diodes (LEDs), both of which burn very coolly (unlike conventional bulbs). They also have long lives, especially LEDs which last for an astonishing 30,000 hours.

22

Use paper towels made from 100% recycled materials.

The manufacture of new towels takes an incredible amount of resources and energy (if all US citizens gave up one roll per year, they would save 1.4 million trees). Better still, switch to cotton or linen towels instead.

23

Shed full of half-empty tins of paint?

Most paint is toxic and difficult to dispose of safely. However, many people would be glad of it. Give your unused (but still usable) paint to a local community group or housing co-operative.

24

Buy only rechargeable batteries. Over 15 billion batteries are produced every year worldwide, and most end up leaking their toxic chemicals inside waste tips. Lithium rechargeables plus a solar-powered charger will last you many months. And where possible buy appliances which use mains electricity.

25

Take holidays which avoid flying.

Use trains, boats and buses instead. This may need more planning, and may cost more (most air fares are unsustainably low), but you won't be responsible for the huge gusts of polluting gases emitted by airliners. Air travel accounts for at least 10% of our climate-changing emissions.

26

Why drink bottled water?

Mains water is miles cheaper and (generally) just as good for you. And it doesn't come in countless millions of plastic bottles which get thrown away. Buy yourself a good quality water bottle and fill that. It will last you for many years.

27

Check the pressure in your car tyres regularly (at least once a month). More than half of all vehicles run on under-inflated tyres, thereby wasting about 5% of their fuel. The correct pressure for your car can be found in the manual.

28

On gardens and paths, **keep weedkillers** for **a last resort.** Most of them contain **very harmful chemicals** which may linger in the soil. Remove weeds by hand or by hoeing. If you absolutely must use a herbicide, buy one containing glyphosate (which very quickly breaks down).

29

Someone, somewhere, wants your old or unused tools.

Give surplus tools to a charity such as Workaid or Tools With a Mission. They will refurbish them and send them to people who need them in developing countries.

30

Turn off the water when you brush your teeth or soap your hands.

The same goes when you are washing dishes in the kitchen sink. Leave the tap running and you waste an incredible amount of water. (Take shorter showers too – five minutes is quite long enough.)

31

If you're sitting outside at night,

warm yourself with a wood fire or a thick coat.

Avoid patio heaters,

which are fantastically wasteful gadgets.
One heater produces more toxic gas than a car
– and anyway, how can you heat the open air?

32

Shave with an electric razor, or use one with extractable blades. Disposable razors last only a short time before they get thrown away, thereby wasting an amazing amount of plastic and metal. Better still, buy yourself an old-fashioned cut-throat razor which can be regularly sharpened.

33

Some clothes are labelled

dry clean only.

By and large, it's safe to ignore this.
Dry cleaning involves some very nasty chemicals indeed, some of which have been linked to cancer and other ailments, so

avoid it.
Instead, try gently washing

the garments in a mild detergent and then air-drying them.

34

Harvest the rain. Water is a precious resource. Anything which comes free should be cherished and stored in butts or cisterns. Non-drinkable **rain water** can be used **for many things,** from watering the garden to filling the washing machine. Modern systems make this simpler than ever. Just look up 'rain harvesting'.

35

Use recycled timber for floors, cupboards and shelving. You may have to remove old nails and paint, but by reusing you will spare several trees from the chainsaw. And the quality of the wood will probably be better than anything you can buy new. There's a building materials reclamation site somewhere near you.

36

Improve the natural light in your home

– and save on electricity. Wooden window frames have thinner bars than plastic ones, and therefore a bigger area of glass. Roof windows (or skylights) are even better, because they let in more direct light from above. Best of all, install an aluminium 'light tube'.

37

Let the grass grow. Our obsession with beautifully manicured lawns drives us to overuse our gas-guzzling mowers, not to mention fertilizers, weedkillers and water sprinklers. So, keep your grass a little longer by **cutting** it **less often.** Sow patches with wildflower seeds and forget about the chemicals.

38

Extend the life of your computer.

Two thirds of a computer's environmental cost lies in its manufacturing. So put off buying a new one and upgrade the old one to make it last longer. You can triple the size of the memory simply by buying a stick and plugging it inside the PC where indicated (but read the manual first).

39

Burn locally-produced charcoal on your barbecue,

preferably from coppiced woodland (which renews itself quickly). Avoid buying barbecue briquettes, which usually contain a quickfire chemical which will taint the food and pollute the air.

40

Buy food and other goods with as little packaging as possible. Packaging wastes resources and spoils the environment (and its cost will be added to the price). If you're feeling really bold, remove the excess packaging and leave it in the shop. Or go to farmers' and other markets, where goods are weighed out loose.

41

Is your carpet really necessary?

Most modern carpets are made of synthetic materials which need a lot of energy to make, and may contain harmful chemicals. Just like wool carpets, they harbour dust mites and fleas and demand regular vacuum cleaning. Settle for a timber floor with a few (easily-shakeable) rugs.

42

Eat food that has been grown organically.

It may taste better and it may be more healthy for you – but that's not the real point. Organic growing methods do no harm to the soil and other parts of the ecosystem. Inorganic methods, using a vast battery of chemicals, do a lot of harm. That's why you should eat organic.

43

Always run your washing machine with a full load. Half-loads waste water and power, whatever manufacturers say. At the same time, set the running temperature as low as possible – 40°C is plenty hot enough for most purposes.

44

Install a wood-burning stove. These are usually made of cast iron, which radiates heat amazingly well and lasts forever. And they burn firewood, which is an easily renewable resource. It's a much cheaper and more environmentally friendly way of heating a room than a gas- or oil-fired boiler. And it smells a lot better.

45

Plant at least one broad-leaved tree a year.

Trees are a vital cog in our delicate environmental machine, and they are disappearing fast. Plant new ones for future generations to thank you for. If your own garden is too small, you can compensate by giving trees as gifts to others.

46

Delete computer software that is not strictly necessary.

Much of this is smuggled into your PC bundled up with free downloads, and is programmed to be 'always on', thereby putting more strain on the computer and shortening its life by as much as two years. Go to 'Control Panel' and delete as many as you can.

47

Think hard before buying fish to eat.

Due to monstrous over-fishing, the populations of many well-known species are in danger of collapse. These include tuna, cod, monkfish, haddock, swordfish, skate and shark. In their place, choose the likes of herring, mackerel, pollack and sea-farmed salmon.

48

Get a meter fitted to your water supply.

Fixed water charges tend to make us lazy. When you realize exactly how much your water costs, you will quickly start to use less – and pay less. All of which is good for the environment.

49

Buy yourself a portable electricity monitor.

This simple gadget shows how much electricity you're using, and how much it is costing you. It is also a much handier alternative to watching the meter in the cupboard. The shock of knowing your actual consumption can lead you to cut a big slice off electricity bills.

50

Become an independent shopper. The power and influence of supermarkets have grown to amazing proportions. They are able to operate in ways which have a direct (and often lamentable) effect on the environment. Break **free of** the **supermarket chains** and support local producers, farm shops and co-operatives.

William Fortt

William Fortt is a keen environmentalist who delights in minimizing personal waste and helping to heighten people's awareness of pollution. He is also an experienced gardener, whose cottage garden in Wiltshire is famed for the beauty of its rare plants and the wonders of its many varieties of culinary and medicinal herbs. He has been an author for more than 30 years, with many books to his name.

THE LITTLE BOOK OF
BARBECUE
TIPS
ANDREW LANGLEY

THE LITTLE BOOK OF
BEER
TIPS
ANDREW LANGLEY

THE LITTLE BOOK OF
HERB
TIPS
WILLIAM FORTT

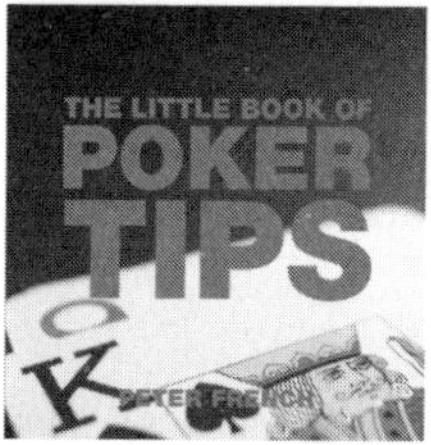
THE LITTLE BOOK OF
POKER
TIPS
PETER FRENCH

THE LITTLE BOOK OF
GARDENING
TIPS
WILLIAM FORTT

THE LITTLE BOOK OF
CHEFS'
TIPS
RICHARD MAGGS

THE LITTLE BOOK OF
SPICE
TIPS
ANDREW LANGLEY

THE LITTLE BOOK OF
GOLF
TIPS
PETER FRENCH

THE LITTLE BOOK OF
TIPS
SERIES

THE LITTLE BOOK OF
CHEESE
TIPS
ANDREW LANGLEY

THE LITTLE BOOK OF
WINE
TIPS
ANDREW LANGLEY

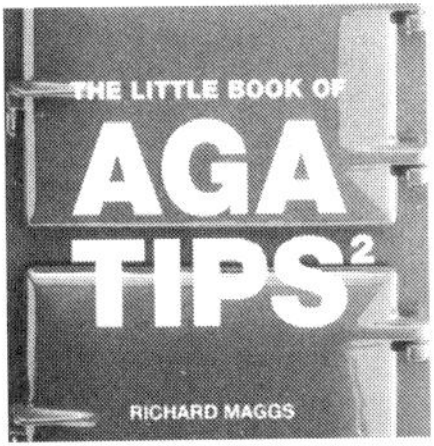
THE LITTLE BOOK OF
AGA
TIPS 2
RICHARD MAGGS

THE LITTLE BOOK OF
COFFEE
TIPS
ANDREW LANGLEY

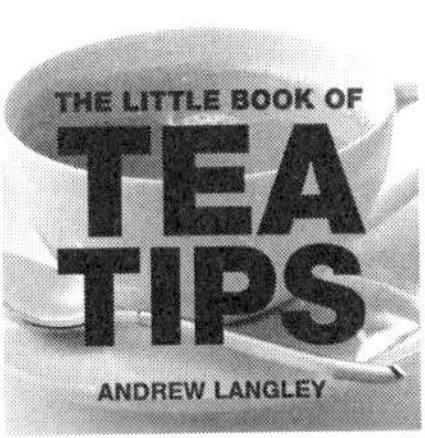
THE LITTLE BOOK OF
TEA
TIPS
ANDREW LANGLEY

THE LITTLE BOOK OF
AGA
TIPS 3
RICHARD MAGGS

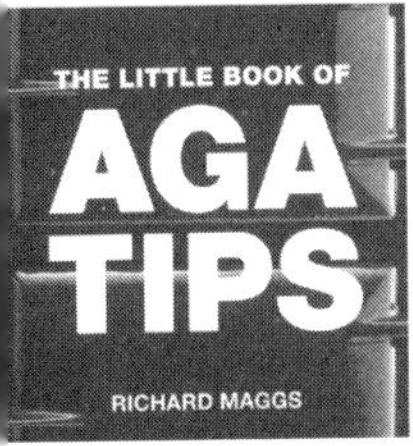
THE LITTLE BOOK OF
AGA
TIPS
RICHARD MAGGS

THE LITTLE BOOK OF
CHRISTMAS
AGA
TIPS
RICHARD MAGGS

THE LITTLE BOOK OF
RAYBURN
TIPS
RICHARD MAGGS

THE LITTLE BOOK OF
BRIDGE
TIPS

THE LITTLE BOOK OF
CHESS
TIPS
PETER FRENCH
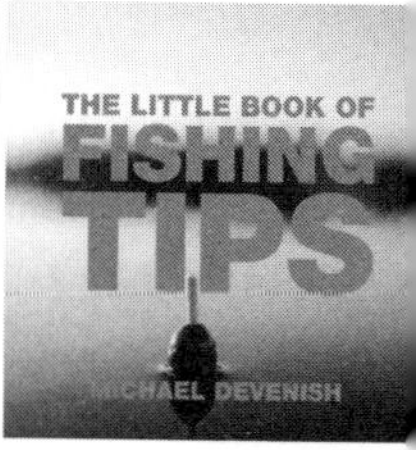
THE LITTLE BOOK OF
FISHING
TIPS

THE LITTLE BOOK OF
GREEN
TIPS
WILLIAM FORTT

THE LITTLE BOOK OF
KITTEN
TIPS
ANDREW LANGLEY

MARMITE
PAUL HARTLEY
THE LITTLE BOOK OF
MARMITE
TIPS
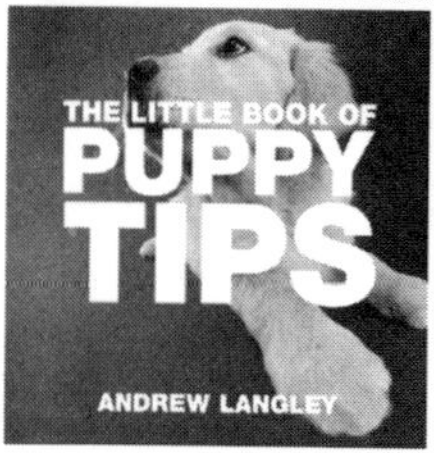
THE LITTLE BOOK OF
PUPPY
TIPS
ANDREW LANGLEY

THE LITTLE BOOK OF
WHISKY
TIPS
ANDREW LANGLEY

THE LITTLE BOOK OF
TRAVEL
TIPS
MEGAN DEVENISH